How Ma

by Michèle Dufresne

Pioneer Valley Educational Press, Inc.

I can see **3** kittens.
Can you?

I can see **7** swans.
Can you?

I can see 1 panda.
Can you?

I can see 4 pigs.
Can you?

I can see 9 ducks.
Can you?

I can see **2** horses.
Can you?

I can see 5 puppies.
Can you?

How Many?

ducks

kittens

horses

panda

pigs

puppies

swans